THE WINTER
HORSE CARE
HANDBOOK

Practical Tips to Keep Horses Healthy, Warm,
and Thriving Through the Cold Months

Emma Caldwell

Table Of
Contents

INTRODUCTION: THE CHANGING SEASON

Understanding Nature's Rhythm and Preparing for a Season of Partnership

The first frost arrives quietly...

One morning the water buckets wear a thin glaze of ice, and every breath from the horses hangs in the air like smoke. The barn smells different now, a mix of hay, leather, and cold wood. Somewhere in the pasture, a mare shifts her weight and blows softly into the chill. The light is lower, the air sharper. The season is turning, and every horse feels it before we do.

Winter horse care begins here, not with panic or heavy blankets, but with observation. Horses are far more capable of thriving in cold weather than most people realize. Nature has prepared them well. Our responsibility is to understand that preparation and support it with thoughtful management.

Nature's Design

How Horses Stay Warm Naturally

When daylight fades and the air cools, a horse's body begins a quiet transformation. Long before we reach for a jacket, their internal systems are adjusting to the coming cold. The sleek summer coat thickens and becomes layered. Beneath the outer guard hairs, which are coarse and waterproof, grows a dense undercoat that traps warm air near the skin. Those outer hairs can stand upright to create an insulating layer, a process called piloerection. This ability turns a horse's coat into a living blanket that adapts to changing weather.

Inside, even more is happening. A horse's natural comfort zone for temperature, is lower than most humans expect. Healthy adult horses with a full, dry coat can remain comfortable at temperatures below freezing. Only when their coat becomes wet or when wind penetrates that insulating layer do they start to lose heat faster than they can produce it. A clipped or thin-coated horse may need help at 10 degrees while a fuzzy pony might be content at zero.

The circulatory system also plays a role. Tiny blood vessels near the skin tighten to conserve heat, keeping the core organs warm. The large muscles of the shoulders and hindquarters generate heat through steady movement, which is one reason regular turnout is so beneficial even in winter. Inside the digestive tract, slow fermentation of forage in the hindgut creates steady internal warmth. Each mouthful of hay becomes a small fuel log for the body's internal furnace. More forage means more heat.

Behaviorally, horses adapt too. They turn their hindquarters toward the wind, stand close to one another for shared warmth, and seek shelter only when weather becomes both wet and cold. Over several weeks, their bodies gradually adjust to each drop in temperature. Acclimatization is a process, not an event, and it allows the horse to remain comfortable during winter.

When you see a horse standing peacefully in a snowy field with unmelted flakes resting on its back, you are witnessing that system at work. The snow remains because the coat's insulation prevents heat from escaping. The horse is not freezing; it is comfortable and perfectly adapted to its climate.

How Horses Generate Warmth

- **Forage Fermentation:** Fiber digestion produces steady heat in the hindgut.
- **Muscle Activity:** Even gentle movement increases circulation and core temperature.
- **Insulation:** A fluffy coat traps air and reduces heat loss.
- **Fat Reserves:** Horses develop a modest fat layer that buffers against cold.
- **Behavior:** Positioning, posture, and grouping all help conserve energy.

Recognizing the Horse's Comfort

A horse that is warm and well regulated will show:
- Relaxed posture with one hind leg resting
- Normal breathing and no shivering
- Dry, warm skin under the coat
- Bright eyes and interest in surroundings

A cold horse may appear tense, tuck its tail, or shiver lightly. Persistent shivering or stiffness means it is time to step in with extra forage, shelter, or a blanket.

Understanding these natural systems replaces guesswork with observation and anxiety with respect. It lays the foundation for confident, balanced winter care.

Mindset Shift

From Worry to Wisdom

Many horse owners greet the first cold snap with dread. Shorter days bring frozen hoses, icy footing, and endless blanket changes. Yet winter is not the enemy. True winter care is less about battling the elements and more about adjusting our rhythm and expectations.

The first shift is realizing that horses experience temperature differently than we do. A person in a heavy coat at forty degrees may feel chilled, but a healthy horse with a full coat often finds that temperature refreshing. Our comfort is not the measure of theirs. Learning to read the horse's signals leads to better decisions than acting on our own perception of cold.

A second shift comes from preparation.

The best horsekeepers begin winter work
before the frost arrives.

Fences are repaired, water heaters tested, hay stacked, and shelters checked. With planning, winter becomes predictable and calm instead of frantic. A little work in autumn means peace of mind when snow starts to fall.

Finally, balance is key. Horses thrive when they can move, eat, and think, regardless of temperature. Too much warmth can cause sweating and skin irritation. Too little movement leads to stiffness and restlessness. Every decision, from blanketing to turnout, should support equilibrium rather than comfort one extreme.

Observation Over Anxiety

Observation is a horsekeeper's greatest winter tool.
Each horse has unique needs based on age, body condition, and coat type. Some thrive outdoors, while others prefer a shelter during harsh wind. None of these differences are problems if we learn to read them. The goal is not identical treatment for every horse, but attentive care for each one.

Observation builds confidence. When you can recognize the signs of comfort and stress, you spend less time guessing and more time enjoying your horse. The shift from fear to familiarity is one of the most rewarding parts of becoming a skilled winter caretaker.

The Winter Partnership

Working With the Season

Winter invites a new kind of partnership between horse and human. It requires patience, awareness, and dependable routine. We provide structure, feed, and shelter. The horse, in return, teaches steadiness and resilience.

Partnership begins with trust. When you place your hand on a horse's thick coat and feel warmth beneath, you are reminded that nature already has a plan. Your role is not to replace that plan, but to enhance it. You watch the coat for dullness or dampness, check water for ice, and learn each horse's daily rhythm. These small acts deepen understanding and form the heart of true horsemanship.

Routine builds security. Horses thrive on consistency. Feeding at regular times, keeping water available, and maintaining safe footing communicate reliability and safety. At the same time, winter care calls for flexibility. One day may require an extra flake of hay, another a rest from turnout because of glare ice. True partnership is responsive rather than rigid.

The Quiet Season of Connection

In the stillness of winter, the bond between horse and caretaker grows stronger. The barn hums with the soft sounds of chewing hay and contented sighs. Winter slows everything down, inviting us to notice details we miss in busier seasons. A horse senses our calmness. When we move with quiet confidence, it relaxes and follows our lead. Winter care becomes less about tasks and more about rhythm - the cold mornings, the crack of ice, and the glow of yellow light - all become part of this shared experience.

Daily Winter Observation Checklist

- Check water temperature and ensure it is not frozen.
- Run your hand through the coat to confirm it is dry and warm.
- Observe mood and appetite.
- Feel limbs for warmth and suppleness.
- Note changes in manure or urine output.
- Confirm safe footing in turnout areas.

Partnership begins with trust.

An Invitation to the Season Ahead

Winter is not a pause in horse life; it is a transformation. It teaches us to move more slowly, to plan ahead, and to appreciate the rituals of care. It sharpens our observation, deepens empathy, and reminds us that comfort grows from partnership rather than control.

In the chapters ahead, you will explore every element of this season: managing pastures and shelters, adjusting feed, protecting hooves, and maintaining both body and mind. Each chapter builds on this foundation of understanding how horses adapt and how we can meet them in balance with the natural world.

Step outside and breathe the crisp air. Watch your horse turn its head toward you, nostrils steaming in the morning light. The season has changed, but your connection remains, stronger than ever.

Winter has arrived, and your partnership begins here.

CHAPTER 1: MANAGING PASTURE AND SHELTER

Creating safe, healthy outdoor environments for horses in winter.

Reader Takeaways
- Build and maintain mud-free turnout areas.
- Ensure fresh air and healthy ventilation without drafts.
- Design windbreaks and run-ins for comfort and safety.
- Manage snow, ice, and drainage to keep footing firm.

Winter challenges every horse keeper with frozen ground, slick gateways, and icy troughs. This chapter explains how to prepare and maintain pastures, paddocks, and shelters so that horses stay comfortable, sound, and secure through the coldest months.

1. Preparing Before Frost

Reading the Land

Walk your property after autumn rain. Note where water pools and where it drains. Those wet zones become skating rinks once temperatures drop. Mark high, well-drained ground for winter turnout and feeding.

Sketch paddocks, gates, and waterers. Circle high-traffic areas and plan a sacrifice paddock to spare your main pasture. Place it near the barn for easy access but far enough from waterways to prevent runoff contamination.

Tip: A paddock on slightly elevated ground saves spring pastures and keeps horses cleaner all winter.

Building All-Weather Pads

Mud control begins with preparation. At gates, feeders, and water points, build a heavy-use pad:
1. Excavate organic topsoil to firm subgrade.
2. Lay geotextile fabric.
3. Add 4–6 inches of angular stone.
4. Top with 2 inches of screenings and compact firmly.

These layers drain water and create traction. Commercial mud-control grids work well where excavation is difficult. Always crown the center slightly so water flows off both sides.

These layers drain water and create traction. Commercial mud-control grids work well where excavation is difficult. Always crown the center slightly so water flows off both sides.

Water Access and Winterization

Frozen water limits health faster than cold itself. Choose from three main systems:
1. Automatic frost-free waterers set below the frost line.
2. Heated stock tanks or buckets for flexible use.
3. Insulated troughs with float lids in milder regions.

Protect cords in conduit and plug into GFCI outlets. Check flow and temperature twice daily. Drain hoses after every use. Keep pads beneath troughs dry with gravel to prevent icy build-up.

Fencing and Footing Safety

Inspect electric lines and tighten before snow. Add visibility tape where white wire disappears against drifts. Around feeders, use angular gravel rather than round pea stone for traction. Avoid salt; use sand instead.

Ventilation in Shelters

A barn should be no more than a few degrees warmer than outdoors. Install eave inlets and ridge vents to create an upward airflow. Moist, stagnant air causes more harm than cold air. Condensation or ammonia odor means the system is failing. Strip wet bedding daily and keep airflow steady.

What Is a Sacrifice Paddock?

A small, surfaced turnout area used in wet or frozen weather so the main pasture can rest. It prevents erosion, keeps hooves dry, and simplifies feeding near the barn.

Preparation turns winter from struggle to routine. Gravel laid in October and vents opened in November become the quiet heroes of February comfort. Each small effort now prevents crisis later.

> Winter care is not about fighting the elements; it is about arranging them to work with you.

2. Daily Maintenance

Establish a Winter Rhythm

Consistency prevents accidents. Inspect paddocks twice daily using the same route: gates, footing, water, fencing. Fifteen minutes of observation saves hours of repair.

Turnout Management

Use the sacrifice lot daily and rest larger fields. Maintain smooth walking paths through snow. Spread multiple hay piles to reduce competition. Rotate turnout groups if space is tight.

Barn and Shelter Housekeeping

Remove manure and wet bedding each morning. Replace with dry material to absorb moisture. Open eave vents if condensation appears. Ammonia odor means ventilation failure, not simply dirty stalls.

Water and Ice Checks

Inspect troughs morning and evening. Ice thicker than a coin signals poor heating. Break crusts gently with a plastic scoop. Horses drink best when water stays near 45 °F. Offer soaked feeds if intake drops.

Entry and Exit Safety

Scrape compacted snow and apply sand or wood ash for traction. Avoid rock salt near shoes or leather. Oil hinges weekly so cold metal does not seize.

Manure and Runoff Management

Remove manure daily from high-traffic zones. Stockpile on a raised, covered pad at least 100 ft from water. During thaws, check that runoff flows away from shelters.

Lighting and Routine Checks

Clean lights and fans weekly. Listen during evening rounds for drips or hissing water lines. Sounds often reveal problems before sight does.

Orderly routines create calm. Clean air, firm footing, and consistent checks turn long winters into manageable seasons.

Winter chores are the daily proof of care. Do them steadily and spring arrives as reward, not rescue.

3. Windbreaks and Run-Ins

Understanding Wind Chill

Cold air alone rarely harms a healthy horse; wind strips the insulating layer of the coat. A steady breeze that reduces wind speed by half can lower energy loss dramatically. Horses prefer a calm, dry space where they can still breathe fresh air.

Designing Windbreaks

Effective windbreaks are semi-porous, about 60–70 percent dense. They slow air instead of blocking it.
Key Points
- Align perpendicular to prevailing winter winds.
- Extend ends beyond the protected area by 1.5 times the height.
- Height of 10–12 ft suits most horses.
- Use evergreen rows or slatted fences with small gaps.
- Maintain drainage under the barrier to prevent meltwater pooling.

Integrating with Pastures

Windbreaks can divide large pastures or protect feeding zones. Combine fast-growing and long-lived trees for durability. Protect young trunks from chewing with temporary fencing until mature.

Run-In Shed Design

Face openings away from prevailing winds, usually south or southeast. Keep bedding dry and replace wet areas daily.

Flooring and Bedding

Gravel floors with straw or coarse shavings stay firm and dry. On bare dirt, install mats or geotextile fabric before bedding. Remove frozen clumps regularly to maintain safe footing.

Snow and Ice Around Shelters

After storms, clear entrances and throw snow downwind. Maintain a cleared buffer around buildings. Check roofs for load and rake from the ground if snow exceeds six inches. Never pile snow against wood siding or gates.

Workflow and Access

Locate feeders and waterers within the sheltered zone but outside the shed. Keep human routes downwind to avoid drifts.

Ideal Run-In Shelter Design
Three-sided, open south, crowned gravel floor, eave and ridge vents, roof overhang, gravel apron, snow-drift pattern shown.

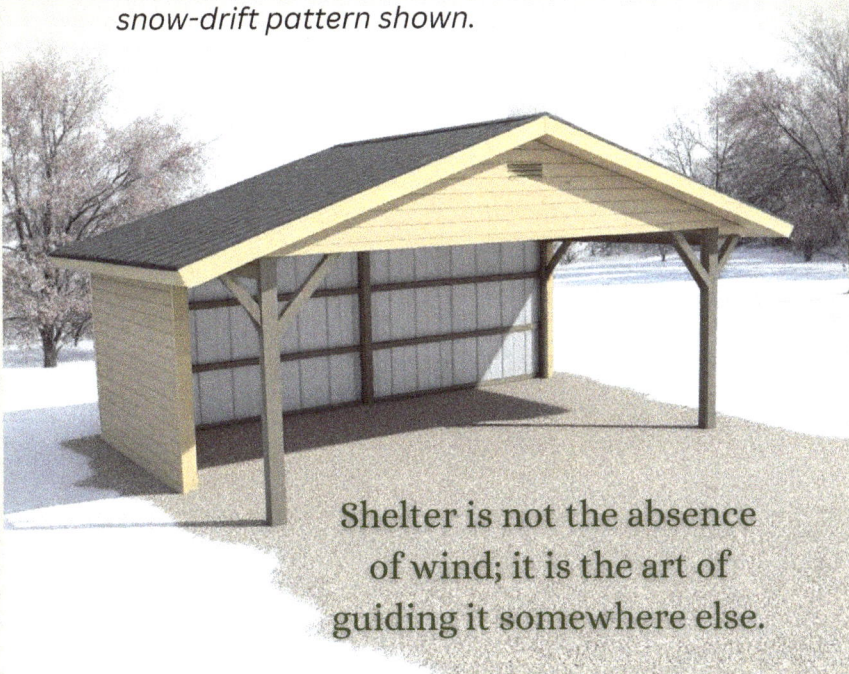

Shelter is not the absence
of wind; it is the art of
guiding it somewhere else.

4. Snow, Ice, and Drainage

Design for Thaw Cycles

A slope of 1–2 percent guides meltwater away from shelters. Crown pad centers and lead runoff toward vegetated buffers. Clear swales of debris before freeze. Each inch of elevation gained now saves a foot of mud later.

Management of Ice

Use traction, not melting, for safety.
Preferred materials: coarse sand, wood ash, poultry grit.
Apply lightly each morning. For concrete, choose calcium-magnesium acetate or urea de-icer. Avoid salt and never mix it with manure.

Snow Management Around Barns

After storms, clear entrances first and push snow downwind. Keep a 3–5 ft buffer around buildings. Stack snow where it drains safely. Remove roof loads before they exceed structural limits. Use snow fences upwind to catch drifting snow.

Footing and Freeze Management

Remove manure daily and level surfaces before night freezes. Plow narrow walking lanes rather than entire paddocks. Apply hoof wax or petroleum jelly to prevent ice balls under shoes.

Managing Meltwater and Runoff

During early thaws, create shallow gravel trenches to move water away from gates. Keep bedding and manure piles on high pads. Close off saturated zones until they refreeze to avoid deep ruts.

Snow and ice are temporary if water has somewhere to go. Guide it, channel it, and respect its power. When spring comes, dry paddocks and clean shelters will reward every winter effort.

Checklist for Barn Winterization

A. Structural Preparation

- ☐ Inspect **roof, gutters, and downspouts** for leaks and blockages. Clear leaves and debris before first snow.
- ☐ Check **siding, doors, and windows** for gaps; seal only enough to stop drafts at human height—maintain airflow above stalls.
- ☐ Service **run-in sheds**: verify roof integrity, reinforce loose boards, and grade entrances for drainage.
- ☐ Examine **floors and mats** for wear or heaving; re-level uneven stall bases.
- ☐ Confirm **barn lighting** functions; replace burned-out bulbs with enclosed, dust-proof fixtures.

B. Ventilation and Air Quality

- ☐ Open and clean **eave and ridge vents**; remove bird nests, cobwebs, or dust.
- ☐ Check that each stall has at least one **fresh-air opening** not directly on the horse.
- ☐ Test humidity: no condensation on windows or roof panels.
- ☐ Establish a routine for **daily manure removal and bedding checks** to reduce ammonia.

C. Electrical and Heating Safety

- ☐ Test all **GFCI outlets** and label those powering heated buckets or tank de-icers.
- ☐ Inspect cords and plugs for cracks or chew marks; route through conduit or protective tubing.
- ☐ Keep **extension cords** off floors and away from bedding.
- ☐ Mount any **heat lamps or space heaters** well clear of hay or dust; use only farm-rated equipment.
- ☐ Store **fire extinguishers** in visible, accessible spots; confirm gauges show full charge.

D. Water Systems

- ☐ Drain and insulate **outdoor hydrants** and exposed pipes.
- ☐ Test **automatic waterers** for flow and heater function.
- ☐ Place **heated buckets** on level surfaces with cords secured behind protective fencing.
- ☐ Keep a backup **hose stored indoors** for refilling during deep freezes.
- ☐ Confirm all horses have access to **lukewarm (40–50 °F)** water daily.

E. Feed and Forage

- ☐ Stock **60–90 days of hay** under cover, stacked on pallets with airflow.
- ☐ Rotate stacks so oldest hay is used first.
- ☐ Secure **grain bins** against rodents; inspect for moisture or mold.
- ☐ Keep a **salt block or loose salt** accessible in each turnout area.

F. Shelter and Turnout

- ☐ Grade or add **gravel pads** at gates, waterers, and feeders to prevent mud and ice.
- ☐ Set up **windbreaks** or slatted panels facing prevailing winds.
- ☐ Check **run-in shed drainage** and roof overhangs.
- ☐ Maintain **sand or stone-dust bins** near each gate for traction.
- ☐ Install reflective **markers or lights** on paths used after dark.

G. Equipment and Supplies

- ☐ Service **tractors, wheelbarrows, and spreaders**; check tires and batteries.
- ☐ Stock **shovels, roof rakes, ice chisels, and snow pushers**.
- ☐ Keep a **first-aid kit** for horses and humans up to date.
- ☐ Prepare a **storm supply tote** with flashlights, spare halters, lead ropes, and extra bedding.
- ☐ Verify **generator operation** and store fresh fuel safely.

H. Manure and Drainage

- ☐ Empty or relocate **manure piles** away from runoff paths.
- ☐ Build or maintain a **gravel or geotextile base** under storage sites.
- ☐ Plan winter access for hauling even in snow; mark driveways and gates with tall stakes.

I. Record-Keeping and Routine

- ☐ Post **emergency contacts** near barn phone and entrance.
- ☐ Create a **daily winter checklist** for staff or volunteers.
- ☐ Note **body-condition scores** and weight estimates before cold sets in.
- ☐ Schedule **mid-winter maintenance day** for mid-season tune-ups.

If workload remains moderate to heavy during winter, add a low-starch concentrate or high-fat pellet.

CHAPTER 2: WINTER FEEDING STRATEGIES

Balancing calories, fiber, and hydration when the pasture sleeps

Reader Takeaways
- Estimate winter calorie needs and adjust feed by temperature and workload.
- Select and store hay safely for consistent nutrition.
- Supplement with concentrates and minerals only where necessary.
- Encourage adequate water consumption despite freezing conditions.
- Monitor body condition and digestion week by week.

When frost seals the grass, nutrition becomes a deliberate craft. Horses evolved to graze continuously on fibrous forage; winter disrupts that rhythm. This chapter explains how to replace lost pasture nutrients, keep water flowing, and prevent the seasonal pitfalls of weight loss, impaction colic, and metabolic flare-ups.

1. Understanding the Winter Energy Equation

Cold itself is not the enemy; energy imbalance is.

A mature horse at maintenance begins using extra calories to maintain body heat when **the ambient temperature drops below the lower critical temperature** - typically around 40 °F (4 °C) for a well-haired horse, and closer to 50 °F (10 °C) for a clipped or thin animal.

Rule of thumb: For every 10 °F (6 °C) below the LCT, **increase feed energy by about 2–3 percent**. For a 1,100-pound horse, that means one to two extra flakes of average grass hay.

The safest way to provide those calories is through **fiber,** not fat or grain. Digestion of roughage in the hindgut releases heat, a natural furnace from within. Concentrates add energy efficiently but generate less warmth and can upset microbial balance when overfed.

Note: Healthy adult horses in light work can thrive through winter on good-quality hay alone if intake and water access remain adequate.

🔥 The Internal Heating System

Forage fermentation in a horse's hindgut creates a natural internal heating system. When horses digest fiber-rich hay and grass, beneficial microbes in their cecum and large intestine break down cellulose through fermentation, producing heat as a metabolic byproduct.

- **Heat Generation:** Fermentation produces 2-3x more heat than grain digestion
- **Duration:** Heat production continues for 6-8 hours after feeding
- **Location:** Heat is generated internally in the hindgut, warming from inside out
- **Efficiency:** Higher fiber content = more fermentation = more heat

⏰ Fermentation Timeline

Understanding the fermentation process helps optimize feeding schedules. Heat production peaks 2-4 hours after feeding and continues for several hours, making timing crucial for winter warmth.

- **0-2 Hours:** Initial breakdown begins, minimal heat
- **2-4 Hours:** Peak fermentation and heat production
- **4-8 Hours:** Sustained heat generation continues
- **8+ Hours:** Heat production gradually decreases

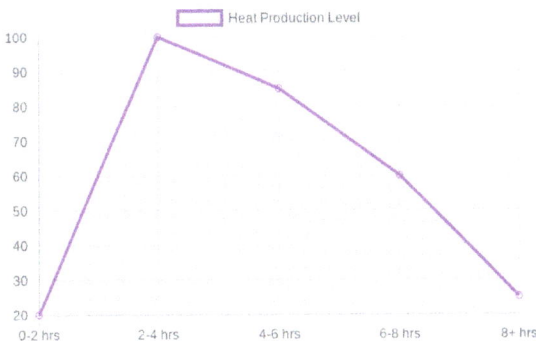

Heat Production Level

| | 0-2 hrs | 2-4 hrs | 4-6 hrs | 6-8 hrs | 8+ hrs |

2. Hay: The Heart of Winter Nutrition

Choose hay that is clean, leafy, and aromatic with minimal dust. Common winter options:

Store hay under cover on pallets with 6 inches of airflow underneath. Stack loosely to avoid spontaneous heating. Check for moldy bales after any mid-winter thaw.

Mold spores and dust aggravate heaves; discard questionable bales completely rather than feeding the outer layers.

Feeding Frequency
Horses prefer continuous forage access. Divide hay into three to four feedings daily or use slow-feed nets or boxes to extend eating time. Constant nibbling keeps the gut moving and the horse warmer.

Hay Allowance Guide
- Minimum: 1.5 % of body weight in dry matter per day
- Typical winter: 2.0–2.5 % for maintenance
- Hard keeper or severe cold: up to 3 % of body weight

For an 1,100-lb gelding, that equals 22–33 lb of hay daily.

Round Bales
Round bales save labor but must be managed carefully. Use bale feeders that keep hay off the ground and limit waste.
Monitor dominant horses so submissive ones are not excluded. Cover the top of the bale or choose net-wrapped versions to prevent rain and snow spoilage.

3. Concentrates and Supplements

When to Add Grain
If weight loss continues despite free-choice hay, or if workload remains moderate to heavy, add a low-starch concentrateor high-fat pellet. Begin with small increments of 0.25 lb per feeding and reassess every 10 days. Rapid feed changes risk digestive upset.

Fat and Fiber Enhancers
Vegetable oils, stabilized rice bran, or beet pulp provide safe calorie boosts.
- Beet pulp: Soak before feeding; offers digestible fiber and moisture.
- Rice bran: Adds fat and phosphorus; balance with calcium.
- Oil: Start with ¼ cup daily and increase slowly.

Vitamins and Minerals
Winter forage lacks fresh-grass vitamins A and E. A ration balancer or loose mineral formulated for your region fills gaps. Salt intake encourages drinking, so keep plain white salt blocks

4. Hydration and Water Management

Cold weather quietly dehydrates horses. When water temperature falls below 45 °F (7 °C), most horses drink less, raising the risk of impaction colic.

Strategies to Maintain Intake
- Use heated buckets or automatic waterers with thermostatic control.
- Offer lukewarm water to encourage consumption.
- Check each water source morning and evening for flow and cleanliness.
- Add 1 tablespoon of salt or electrolytes to feed once daily for horses reluctant to drink.
- Soak hay cubes, pellets, or beet pulp for added moisture.

Monitor manure consistency: dry, hard balls indicate inadequate hydration.

5. Feeding Management in Groups

Winter herds often change hierarchy around limited food sources. Provide at least one hay station per horse plus one extra. Spread piles 10–15 feet apart so all can eat peacefully.

Use hay nets in separate areas for shy horses. Dominant animals will waste less if feeders are abundant.

Feed grains individually to ensure accurate intake and prevent choking. Observe each horse for body condition changes every two weeks.

Feeding through winter is a dialogue between weather, forage, and observation. A horse that chews steadily, drinks freely, and keeps a smooth outline under its coat is proof that the system works. Calories, water, and patience form the quiet rhythm of survival until green returns.

Monitoring Body Condition Week by Week

1. Hands-On Assessment

Use your hands, not your eyes. Thick winter coats hide changes that fingertips detect immediately. Once each week, feel along the ribcage, behind the shoulder, and over the tail head. Note whether ribs are easier or harder to find. Run your palm down the crest of the neck and over the loins; sponginess means fat gain, sharpness means loss. Record these impressions in a notebook or phone log.

"Warmth in winter begins in the hay net and ends in the water bucket."

A Body Condition Score (BCS) chart provides structure:

BCS (1–9)	Meaning	Action
4	Slightly thin; ribs easy to feel	Increase hay by 10–15 %
5	Ideal; ribs felt, not seen	Maintain ration
6	Fleshy; soft fat at tail head	Reduce concentrates slightly

Weekly monitoring builds a rhythm that supports the entire winter care program described in previous chapters. Feeding adjustments, water management, and hoof scheduling all depend on what your records reveal.

📊 Winter Management Strategies

Effective winter horse care combines proper forage selection, feeding schedules, and management practices to maximize the warming benefits of fermentation while maintaining horse health and condition.

- **Free Choice Hay:** Allows horses to eat when cold
- **Evening Feeding:** Provides overnight heat production
- **Shelter Access:** Protects from wind while allowing movement
- **Body Condition:** Monitor weight to adjust feeding

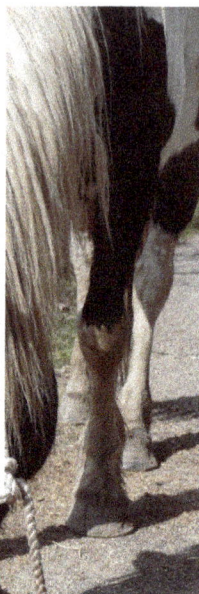

🎯 Key Takeaways

Forage fermentation is nature's heating system for horses. By understanding and optimizing this process, horse owners can help their animals stay warm naturally during cold weather while maintaining health and condition.

Best Practices Summary:

- Increase hay quantity by 20-30% in cold weather
- Choose mature, high-fiber hay for maximum heat
- Feed larger evening meals for overnight warmth
- Ensure constant access to unfrozen water
- Monitor body condition and adjust accordingly
- Provide wind protection while allowing movement

Remember: Forage fermentation is a horse's most efficient natural heating system - fuel it properly for winter success!

CHAPTER 3: HOOF AND LEG CARE IN COLD WEATHER

Keeping hooves healthy amid ice, mud, and reduced exercise

Reader Takeaways
- Understand how cold weather alters hoof growth, moisture, and circulation.
- Prevent frostbite and protect limbs from chill injury.
- Develop daily routines for inspection, cleaning, and hoof care.
- Keep joints flexible and tendons warm during reduced exercise periods.

Hoof and leg health is the foundation of equine soundness, yet winter often works against it. Freezing mud, fluctuating moisture, icy surfaces, and limited movement create a perfect storm for cracks, bruises, and infections. Cold also slows hoof growth and tightens circulation, making small problems linger longer.

1. How Winter Changes the Hoof

Growth and Circulation

Hoof horn grows more slowly in cold weather because blood flow to the extremities decreases as the horse conserves body heat. A typical horse that grows one-quarter inch of wall every month in summer may slow to half that rate in deep winter. Less growth means longer intervals between trimming can distort the balance of the foot.

Schedule farrier visits every six to eight weeks year-round, even if the hoof looks short. Trimming maintains symmetry and prevents small flares from turning into cracks when frozen footing resists give.

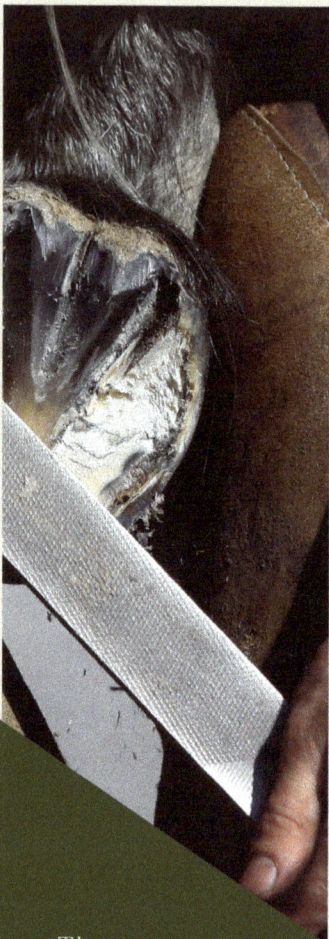

Tip:
Ask your farrier to adjust trim angles slightly steeper for better breakover and traction on hard ground, especially if barefoot.

Moisture Balance

Winter air is dry, yet footing alternates between ice and mud. This combination dehydrates the hoof wall while saturating the sole. The result is brittle, chipping edges above a soft, vulnerable sole.

To maintain balance:
- Use a non-petroleum hoof conditioner two to three times per week when humidity is low.
- Keep stalls clean and dry to prevent bacteria from softened frogs.
- Avoid standing water and deep mud that macerates the hoof capsule.
- Apply a light coat of hoof sealant around the wall if horses stand in wet snow daily.

Stable humidity is better than extremes of soaking and drying. Consistent care preserves elasticity in the hoof wall and reduces cracking in spring.

2. Circulation and Frostbite Prevention

Understanding Circulatory Changes

Cold constricts blood vessels, reducing oxygen delivery to tissues. While horses are less prone to frostbite than humans, the ears, tail, and lower legs remain vulnerable in extreme cold or windchill.

Horses confined without movement lose natural muscle pumping that assists circulation. Encourage turnout and gentle motion daily, even for short periods. Warm-up walks before work increase hoof blood flow and joint lubrication.

Recognizing Early Signs of Cold Stress

Watch for:
- Persistent hoof or leg coldness even after movement
- Pale or mottled skin around pasterns or fetlocks
- Swelling or stiffness after standing on frozen ground
- Reluctance to move or shifting weight frequently

Provide deep bedding in stalls to insulate hooves from frozen floors. For outdoor horses, thick straw or rubber mats in run-ins protect the digital cushion from frostbite.

Circulation Boosters
- Gentle hand massage of lower legs during grooming
- Ten-minute hand-walk before and after exercise
- Boot wraps or quilted standing bandages overnight for seniors or arthritic horses
- Vitamin E and omega-3 supplements to support vascular elasticity (consult vet before adding)

Note: Heat lamps should be used cautiously. Prolonged radiant heat on one area can dry the hoof wall or overheat tendons.

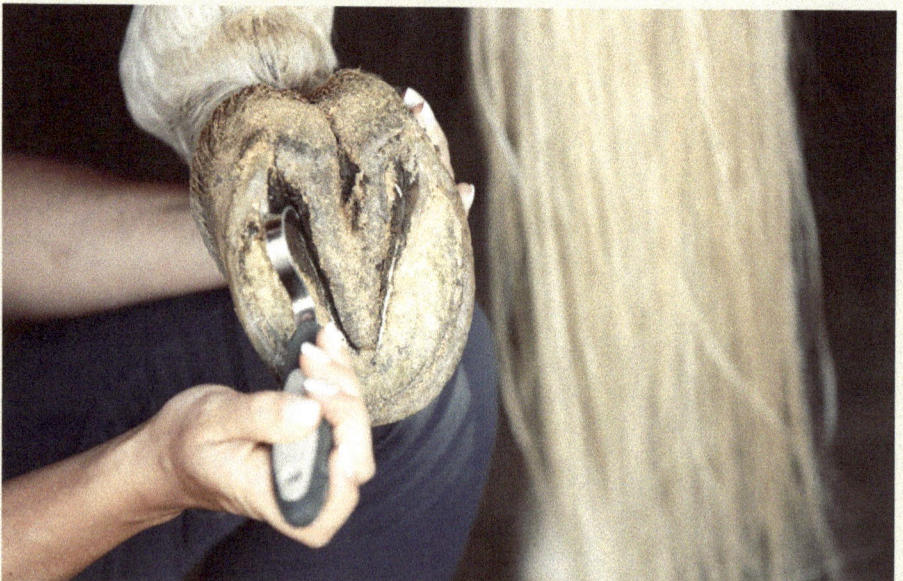

CHAPTER 4: INDOOR TRAINING & EXERCISE

Keeping horses fit and engaged when outdoor work is limited

Reader Takeaways
- Adapt workloads to temperature and footing.
- Practice proper warm-up and cool-down to protect muscles and joints.

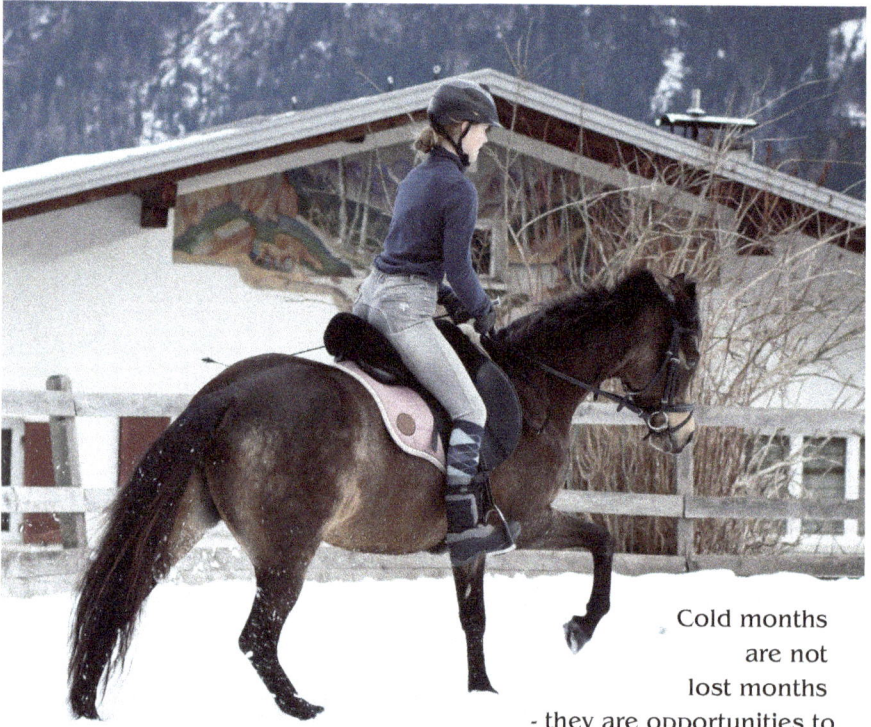

Cold months
are not
lost months
- they are opportunities to
refine balance, flexibility,
and trust.

This chapter guides you in maintaining conditioning and mental sharpness through safe warm-ups, indoor routines, groundwork, and cross-training. With creativity and consistency, even a small indoor space can keep horses sound, supple, and happy until spring.

1. Adjusting Workloads for Cold Weather

Understanding Cold-Weather Physiology

Cold temperatures tighten muscles and reduce joint lubrication. Tendons and ligaments become less elastic until body temperature rises through movement.

The horse that steps briskly into trot on a summer morning may feel resistant or short-strided in winter. Respecting this transition prevents strains and sourness.

Reduce intensity, not purpose. Replace long gallops with collected work, hill sets with pole grids, and extended canter with short bursts of elasticity and rhythm.

For most horses, 20–40 minutes of quality movement is enough to maintain condition when footing limits speed.

Scheduling Work Wisely
- Ride or hand-walk during midday hours, when muscles are warmest and airways least irritated by cold.
- On very cold days, focus on groundwork or stretching instead of heavy schooling.
- Consistency matters more than duration; aim for four or five light sessions weekly rather than one hard workout.

2. Warm-Up and Cool-Down Essentials

The Winter Warm-Up Routine

A correct warm-up is gradual, progressive, and purposeful.
Phase 1 – In-Hand or on the Lunge (5–10 min):
Walk large circles, allow the neck to stretch naturally; do not force a low frame.
Phase 2 – Under Saddle or Extended Work (10–15 min):
Transition frequently between walk and slow trot. Keep strides short and supple. Incorporate lateral flexion and gentle serpentines to encourage bend through cold muscles.
Phase 3 – Working Phase:
Once breathing is steady and muscles feel elastic, begin your chosen exercise plan.

Cooling Down
Allow the same time for cooling as warming. End with 10–15 minutes of relaxed walk, loosening the rein gradually. If the horse has sweated, remove tack promptly and cover with a wicking cooler until coat is dry. Never turn out a damp horse into freezing wind.

Safety Note: Chill after work is a greater risk than cold before it. Dry thoroughly before leaving the arena.

3. Safety and Environmental Factors

Air Quality
Indoor arenas accumulate dust and ammonia quickly in winter. Water footing lightly before riding and maintain ventilation. Use dust-free bedding and avoid sweeping during workouts.

Footing Management
Keep depth consistent - too deep strains tendons, too shallow risks slips. Level and water footing weekly, checking for frozen spots near doors.

Clothing and Tack
Cold leather stiffens; warm tack indoors before use. Use quarter sheets for clipped horses during warm-up and cooling. Choose breathable layers over heavy blankets to prevent sweating.

Winter exercise is less about ambition and more about stewardship. Quiet consistency maintains health, while gentle creativity builds partnership.
A well-planned indoor program produces spring-ready horses that are fitter, calmer, and more balanced than before the snow fell.

CHAPTER 5: COMMON COLD-WEATHER HEALTH RISKS

Identifying, preventing, and treating winter-specific illnesses and injuries

Reader Takeaways
- Keep airways healthy in enclosed barns.
- Reduce colic risk during sudden temperature drops.
- Prevent and treat winter skin and coat problems.
- Recognize warning signs that require veterinary care.

1. Respiratory Concerns in Closed Barns

The Hidden Cost of Warmth

When doors and windows close against the cold, fresh air disappears. Dust from bedding, hay, and manure irritates the lungs, especially in barns with low ceilings. Ammonia from urine compounds the problem by inflaming mucous membranes.
If the air is stale or dusty, the risk of heaves (recurrent airway obstruction) or respiratory infection climbs sharply.

Prevention
- Keep barn humidity below 70 percent with vents open at both eaves and ridge.
- Store hay in a separate loft or shed whenever possible.
- Feed hay at ground level (not from nets above head height) so dust falls away from nostrils.
- Use low-dust bedding such as large-flake shavings or paper.
- Sweep aisles when horses are outside, not during stall time.

Clean air is warmer to the lungs than dusty air will ever be

2. Colic Prevention During Cold Snaps

Why Cold May Cause Colic

Cold weather reduces water consumption, stiffens feed, and limits exercise. These three changes slow gut motility and can lead to impaction colic, the most common winter emergency.

Sudden barometric changes may also alter gut gas production, increasing risk of spasmodic colic.

Prevention Basics

- Keep water above 45 °F (7 °C) with heaters or insulated troughs.
- Offer soaked beet pulp, hay cubes, or warm bran mashes to add moisture.
- Provide plain salt daily to encourage drinking.
- Maintain consistent feeding times; sudden changes in forage type or schedule are major triggers.
- Encourage movement with turnout, hand-walking, or arena exercise.

Early Warning Signs

Pawing, looking at flank - May be gas or impaction pain
Reduced manure or appetite - May be early colic stage
Rolling repeatedly - Severe discomfort
Pale gums or elevated heart rate - Circulatory stress-call vet

Emergency Response

If you suspect colic:
1. Remove all feed but leave water available.
2. Walk the horse gently for 10–15 minutes to stimulate gut motility.
3. Contact your veterinarian if pain persists beyond 30 minutes or vital signs exceed normal.

Never administer pain medication without consulting the vet; it can mask symptoms and delay diagnosis.

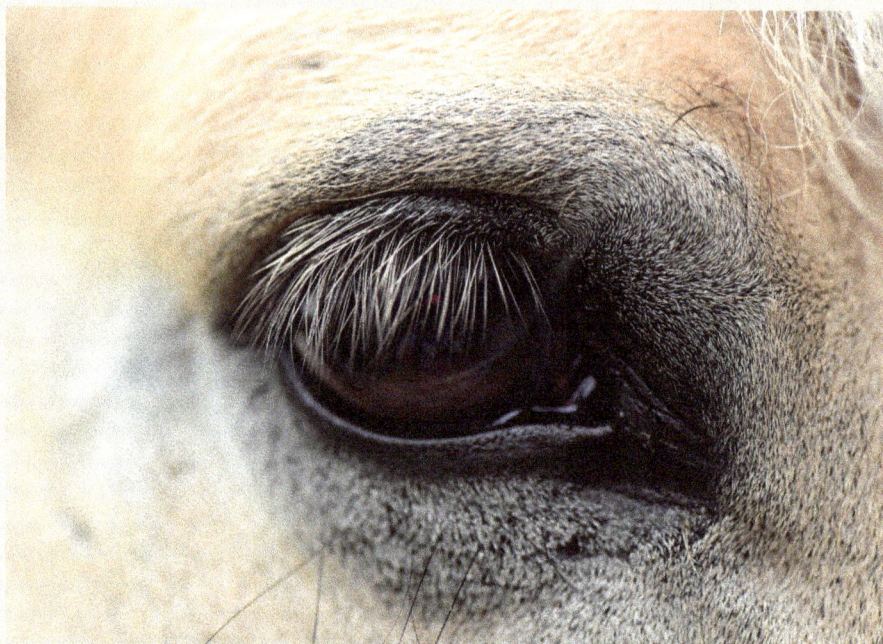

3. Skin and Coat Conditions

Rain Rot and Mud Fever

Even in cold weather, damp conditions under blankets or on legs create bacterial breeding grounds.

Rain Rot (Dermatophilus congolensis)
Appears as crusty scabs along the back or rump. Caused by moisture trapped under heavy coats or blankets.
Treatment: Clip and clean affected area with chlorhexidine solution, dry thoroughly, and expose to air. Disinfect brushes and blankets.

Mud Fever (Pastern Dermatitis)
Found on heels and fetlocks after standing in wet footing.
Treatment: Gently remove scabs, cleanse with antimicrobial wash, and keep legs dry. Apply protective zinc oxide barrier before turnout.

Blanket Rubs and Hair Loss

Improper fit causes shoulder and wither sores.
To prevent:
- Use shoulder guards or silky liners under stable blankets.
- Wash liners weekly to remove sweat salts.
- Adjust straps so blankets sit flat, not tight

Dry Skin and Coat Dullness
Low humidity dries skin oils. Feed flaxseed or a balanced omega-3 supplement to improve coat condition. Curry daily to distribute oils and stimulate circulation. Avoid over-bathing; rinse only when necessary and use mild, moisturizing shampoo.

4. When to Call the Vet: Key Winter Red Flags

Symptom	Possible Cause	Immediate Action
Persistent coughing or nasal discharge	Respiratory infection	Increase ventilation, call vet if >24 hr
Refusal to eat or reduced manure output	Colic or dental pain	Check vitals, remove feed, call vet
Shivering or cold ears despite shelter	Hypothermia	Move to dry shelter, blanket, call vet if persists
Swelling in limbs or digital pulse	Laminitis or injury	Cool area, limit movement, call vet
Unsteady gait or collapse	Severe dehydration or systemic illness	Emergency—call vet immediately

Healthy winter horses share common factors: dry bedding, clean air, abundant forage, constant water, and watchful owners. Prevention is not complicated-it is consistency.

When temperature drops suddenly - increase hay before When you smell ammonia - open vents.   blankets.
When manure changes - check hydration.

Routine observation connects every principle of this book: feeding, shelter, hoof care, and training all support one another through the season.

Winter health management is the quiet art of noticing early. Frost on the window, a cough in the aisle, or a missing manure pile each morning-all are messages waiting to be read.

"Winter illness rarely arrives suddenly;
it whispers first. The good caretaker listens."

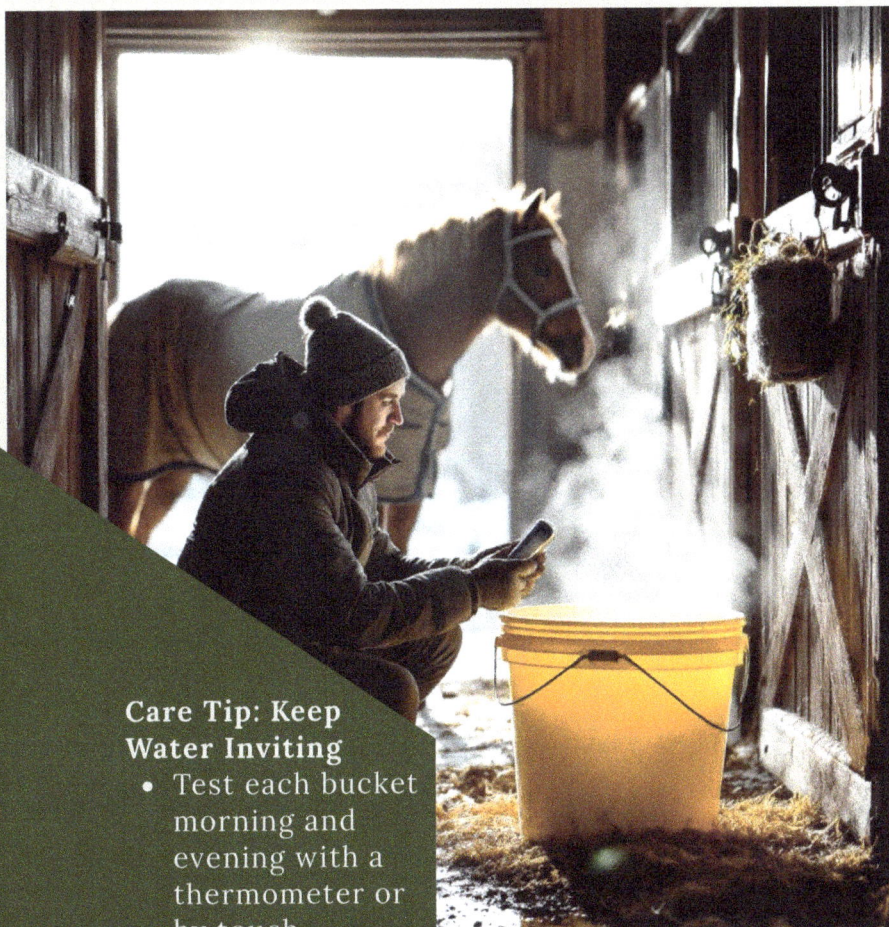

Care Tip: Keep Water Inviting

- Test each bucket morning and evening with a thermometer or by touch.
- Insulate outdoor troughs and check heaters for safe operation.
- Refill with warm water after exercise or late feedings.
- Record daily water use if any horse drinks noticeably less.

Cold weather doesn't just freeze water; it discourages drinking. Horses naturally drink less when the bucket is icy or the surface film turns slushy. Aim for a range of 40–50°F (4–10°C) to match the horse's comfort zone.

DAILY TASKS: Morning & Evening Routine"

Task	Goal / What to Look For	Check
Water sources	Break ice, ensure heaters working, temp 40–50 °F	☐
Feed and hay	Consistent appetite, no refusals or spilled grain	☐
Manure & urine output	Normal quantity, moist texture, not dry or absent	☐
Respiration	Quiet, even, no cough or nasal discharge	☐
Attitude & posture	Bright eyes, alert ears, no shivering or stiffness	☐
Hooves & legs	Pick out hooves, remove snowballs, check for heat or swelling	☐
Blankets	Dry, secure fit, no rubs or damp spots	☐
Bedding	Dry and insulating, no ammonia odor	☐
Airflow	Windows cracked or vents open; no condensation on windows	☐
Temperature record	Note outdoor low/high for the day	☐

Tip: Keep a simple notebook in the tack room for quick notes on any horse that eats, drinks, or moves differently.

WEEKLY TASKS: Prevent, Inspect, Adjust

Task	Purpose	Check
Body Condition Score (BCS)	Feel ribs, tail head, topline for weight changes	☐
Weigh hay and feed portions	Adjust to maintain ideal weight and energy	☐
Clean buckets & troughs	Scrub with brush and rinse with warm water	☐
Ventilation check	Inspect vents, ridge openings, and fans for dust or cobwebs	☐
Stall deep clean	Strip one or two stalls entirely each week	☐
Blanket inspection	Check for wear, broken straps, and proper fit	☐
Grooming day	Thorough curry to check skin and coat for scabs or rubs	☐
Hoof care review	Verify farrier schedule; apply conditioner or sealant	☐
Feed inventory	Confirm hay and bedding stock for at least 2–3 weeks ahead	☐
Tool check	Inspect extension cords, heaters, and water de-icers for wear	☐

Routine cleaning and minor repairs save both money and emergencies later.

MONTHLY TASKS: Evaluate and Refresh

Task	Purpose	Check
Full barn ventilation audit	Open vents, test airflow, remove dust buildup	☐
Health record update	Log weights, vaccines, deworming, dental checks	☐
Farrier visit	Schedule trim or shoe reset every 6–8 weeks	☐
Feed & supplement review	Reassess rations with changing workload or temperature	☐
Blanket wash & rotate	Clean or swap out heavy layers for lighter weights if warming	☐
Emergency supplies check	Refill first-aid kits, batteries, and flashlights	☐
Drainage & footing inspection	Check for ice buildup around gates and paddock pads	☐
Rodent control & storage	Inspect feed bins, sweep storage areas	☐
Vet contact update	Confirm current phone numbers and emergency plan posted	☐

CHAPTER 6: KEEPING YOUR HORSE MENTALLY SHARP IN DOWNTIME

Combatting boredom and anxiety during limited turnout and training

Reader Takeaways
- Create stable enrichment that stimulates curiosity and reduces stress.
- Use safe social turnout or buddy systems to meet herd instincts.
- Deepen trust with daily human-horse rituals that nurture calmness and confidence.

Winter restricts movement, daylight, and routine. These changes challenge not only the horse's body but also the mind. Horses evolved to move, graze, and socialize almost constantly. When those natural behaviors are curtailed, frustration, anxiety, and stable vices often appear.

This chapter explains how to protect mental health through enrichment, social contact, variety, and simple bonding practices that keep your horse bright, calm, and connected through the season of stillness.

1. Enrichment Ideas for the Stabled Horse

Feeding Enrichment

Forage-based enrichment mirrors natural grazing and keeps the gut moving.
Ideas
- Slow feeders or hay nets with varied hole sizes to extend eating time.
- Double-netted hay for longer chew sessions.
- Treat balls or rollers filled with pellets or small carrot pieces.
- Scatter feeding in clean bedding for natural foraging behavior.
- Hanging vegetable strings (carrots, turnips, apples) for gentle challenge.

Rotate methods weekly to maintain novelty. Horses that work for food stay mentally engaged and reduce stress chewing on wood or blankets.

Sensory Enrichment

Appeal to sight, smell, sound, and touch.
- Mirrors: Install unbreakable stable mirrors at chest height; studies show they reduce weaving and anxiety in isolated horses.
- Scent play: Offer safe natural scents (peppermint, chamomile, cinnamon) on cloths or toys once weekly for exploration.
- Music: Soft classical or instrumental music at low volume can calm nervous horses.
- Tactile brushes: Mount textured surfaces or scratch posts at safe height to allow self-grooming.

DIY Toy Ideas

Rope knot toy
Cotton rope tied with treats inside. this toy is for chewing and play

Hanging jug feeder
Plastic milk jug with holes, filled with pellets. Encourages manipulation and problem-solving

Puzzle ball
Old soccer ball with small holes cut. this is for foraging stimulation

Scent towel
Cloth with mild scent
Sensory curiosity

Always supervise during first use. Replace damaged toys to prevent ingestion.

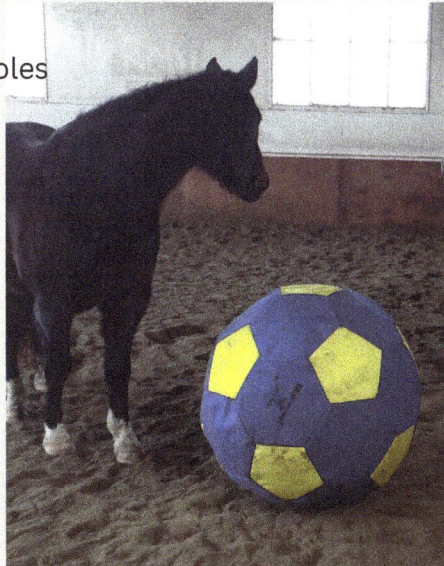

2. Social Time and Safe Companionship

The Social Need

Horses are herd animals; complete isolation is one of the greatest stressors. Even limited physical contact through stall grates or shared turnout reduces cortisol levels and stabilizes heart rate.

Turnout Strategies
- Rotate turnout partners carefully to maintain harmony.
- Choose pairs or small groups based on temperament and hierarchy.
- Provide multiple hay piles to reduce conflict.
- For horses that cannot share space, use adjacent paddocks with visual and vocal contact.

Buddy Systems

Some horses bond with unexpected companions-goats, donkeys, or calm geldings. Companions ease anxiety during storms or when herdmates are away. Ensure companions have compatible diets and safe fencing.

Tip: Social contact is preventive medicine. It lowers heart rate, reduces ulcers, and keeps behavior balanced.

3. Human-Horse Bonding Rituals

Grooming as Connection

Grooming releases endorphins in both horse and handler. Slow curry work stimulates skin oils and circulation. Use grooming time to check for new rubs, scabs, or swelling. End with a quiet moment of stillness, the kind of contact horses value most.

Groundwork Conversations

Practice soft cues, backing a step, yielding to touch, or moving shoulders. Reward attentiveness rather than speed. Five minutes of focused groundwork builds more connection than thirty minutes of mechanical riding.

Quiet Companionship

Simply being present has value. Reading in the stall aisle, offering gentle scratches, or feeding hay by hand during storms reassures anxious horses. Horses remember consistency and calm more vividly than big gestures.

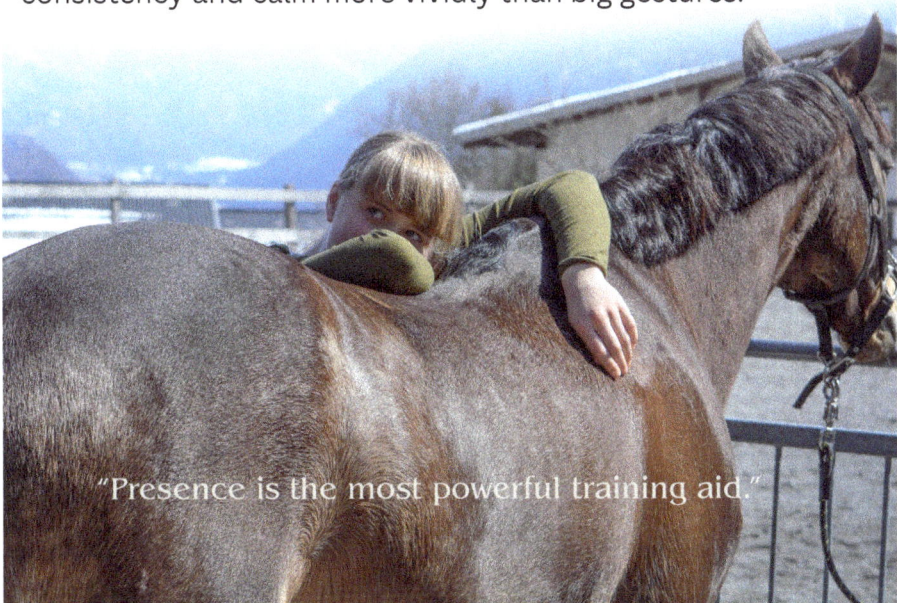

"Presence is the most powerful training aid."

3. Recognizing Mental Fatigue and Boredom

Behavior is communication. Responding to these signals maintains both welfare and safety.

Behavior	Possible Cause	Adjustment
Wood chewing or cribbing	Frustration, lack of forage time	Increase slow-feeder options
Weaving or stall walking	Social isolation	Add mirror or neighbor contact
Ear-pinning at handling	Overstimulation or discomfort	Shorter, calmer sessions
Apathy or dull eyes	Under-stimulation	Add daily puzzle feeder or play
Overexcitement when turned out	Pent-up energy	Increase controlled exercise or hand-walks

A horse's body may slow in winter, but the mind remains hungry for purpose. Every puzzle toy, soft cue, or quiet grooming session tells your horse that life still offers curiosity and companionship even when grass sleeps under snow. Mental enrichment is not luxury; it is welfare.

When the days lengthen again, the horses who stayed mentally engaged through winter step into spring fit in both body and spirit.

"Warmth does not only come from blankets; it grows from attention, play, and trust."

CONCLUSION & YEAR-ROUND READINESS

Carrying winter wisdom into every season

This closing chapter gathers the book's lessons into a philosophy of care — one built on rhythm, respect, and observation — and prepares you to transition smoothly into the seasons ahead.

Winter care is not an isolated season of hardship; it is a masterclass in attention. The same habits that keep horses warm, sound, and content in January form the foundation of year-round health. Clean air, consistent forage, safe footing, and calm routine matter as much in spring mud or summer heat as they do in snow.

1. The Winter Mindset

Observation Over Reaction

Winter teaches patience. You cannot rush water to thaw or hooves to dry; you can only prepare, notice, and adapt. The best caretakers learn to see patterns: how a horse stands when content, how breathing sounds when air is pure, how manure looks when digestion hums.
Observation becomes intuition, and intuition becomes prevention.

"Winter care is not survival; it is the art of noticing early and acting calmly."

Partnership, Not Management

A horse does not think in months or chores; it reads your tone, your timing, and your consistency. Every feeding, grooming, and check is a conversation. Good winter care is a dialogue — one in which trust replaces urgency and steady presence replaces anxiety.

Through the dark months, partnership grows quietly in shared routines: the crunch of hay at dawn, the soft breath in cold air, the rhythm of hooves on frozen ground.

2. Lessons from the Cold Season

Shelter and Pasture

You learned that shelter is not about eliminating wind but guiding it. That dry footing is worth a morning's labor. That clear drainage in autumn saves the pasture in spring.

Keep those principles as the year turns. In summer, shade becomes the windbreak; in rain, drainage paths serve again. Maintenance, not rebuilding, is the reward of good winter groundwork.

Feeding and Hydration

Winter proved that calories and water sustain everything. The horse that drinks and chews stays healthy. Continue weighing hay, checking hydration, and recording intake through every season.

When green returns, transition slowly. Spring grass carries sugars that excite metabolism — the same careful observation that prevented winter colic now prevents spring laminitis.

Hoof and Leg Care

From ice to mud, hooves endure every condition. Winter trimming schedules taught you the value of consistency and attention to moisture balance.

Carry that vigilance forward: in summer, it becomes vigilance against cracks and dryness; in autumn, it becomes preparation for frozen ground once more. The hoof tells the truth about your horse's management all year long.

Health and Prevention

Your winter checklists and observation logs taught you to see early warning signs: small changes in appetite, manure, or mood. Those skills remain vital when heat stress replaces frostbite, or insects replace dust. Prevention is timeless.
Core Principle: Routine saves horses. Crisis interrupts routine; prevention restores it.

3. The Caretaker's Resilience

Just as horses adapt to temperature swings, caretakers adapt to fatigue, frustration, and long nights. Remember to rest, hydrate, and keep your own routines balanced. A tired or hurried handler makes mistakes; a calm, prepared one creates safety.
Celebrate the victories: a healthy coat through the cold, a quiet barn during a storm, a horse that nickers softly when you enter. These are not small successes; they are the proof of good horsemanship.

> "The measure of winter care is not endurance alone but the peace that lingers when it is done."

4. The Return of Light

When you open the barn doors on the first truly warm morning, listen: the same rhythm of breath and hoof that guided you through winter now greets spring. The care, observation, and patience you practiced do not end - they evolve.

Horses carry seasons in their coats, but caretakers carry them in their habits. Each year the work becomes more fluid, the worries fewer, the understanding deeper.

Horses carry seasons in their coats, but caretakers carry them in their habits.

www.ingramcontent.com/pod-product-compliance
Lightning Source LLC
Chambersburg PA
CBHW051249020426
42333CB00025B/3125